Collins
My First book of
The Solar System

Collins My First Book of the Solar System

Collins
An imprint of HarperCollins Publishers
77-85 Fulham Palace Road
London W6 8JB

© HarperCollins Publishers 2011
Maps © Collins Bartholomew Ltd 2011

First published 2011

ISBN 978-0-00-746047-2
ISBN 978-0-00-791027-4

Imp 001

The contents of this edition of Collins My First Book of the Solar System are believed correct at the time of printing.
Nevertheless the publishers can accept no responsibility for errors or omissions, changes in the detail given,
or for any expense or loss thereby caused.

British Library Cataloguing in Publication Data
A catalogue record for this book is available from the British Library.

Printed and bound in Singapore

All mapping in this atlas is generated from Collins Bartholomew digital databases.
Collins Bartholomew, the UK's leading independent geographical information supplier, can provide
a digital, custom, and premium mapping service to a variety of markets. For further information:
Tel: +44 (0) 141 306 3752
e-mail: collinsbartholomew@harpercollins.co.uk

Visit our websites at:
www.harpercollins.co.uk
www.collinsbartholomew.com
www.collinsmaps.com

Contents

Image credits

Introduction

Our Solar System is a busy place, consisting of eight planets, dwarf planets, moons, asteroids, meteoroids, comets, ice and huge amounts of dust and gas that are all travelling around the Sun. *Solar* is a Latin term meaning Sun, and it is this large yellow star that plays an important role in the middle of our Solar System. Due to its size (it contains over 98 per cent of the entire mass of the Solar System), the Sun has a very powerful gravitational pull, attracting all the other planets towards it.

Astronomers have studied the Solar System for thousands of years and are still making new discoveries. The larger, more complex objects that have been discovered are the planets and they all have different characteristics.

There are four inner planets: Mercury, Venus, Earth and Mars. They are said to be terrestrial, in that they are composed mainly of rock, are relatively small, and have few or no moons.

The outer planets include: Jupiter, Saturn, Uranus and Neptune. They are called the Jovian planets. They are large and made up of gas, are ringed, and have many moons.

Pluto was reclassified from a planet to a dwarf planet in 2006. It is actually more like a comet than a planet, with one large moon and three small moons.

The Milky Way

The Milky Way is the name of the
spiral galaxy in which our Solar System
is located. All the stars that we see
in the night sky are part of the Milky
Way galaxy. Aside from the relatively
nearby stars, the galaxy appears as
a hazy band of white light. The Solar
System is located in the Milky Way
halfway out from the centre.

The Solar System

The Milky Way

The Solar System

The Solar System is the Sun and the many objects that orbit it. These objects include eight planets, at least five dwarf planets and countless asteroids, meteoroids and comets. Orbiting some of the planets and dwarf planets are over 160 moons. The Sun keeps its surrounding objects in its orbit by its pull of gravity which has an influence for many millions of kilometres.

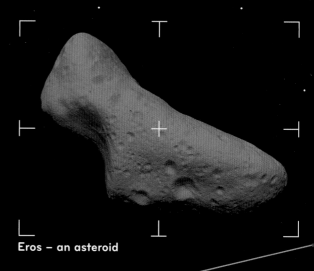

Eros – an asteroid

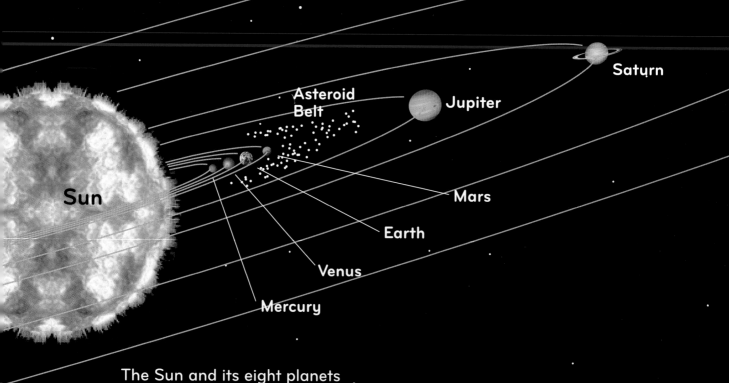

Sun

Asteroid Belt

Jupiter

Saturn

Mars

Earth

Venus

Mercury

The Sun and its eight planets

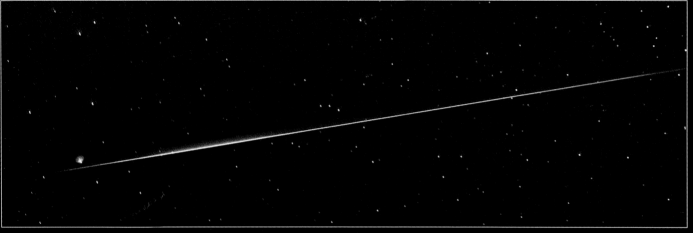

A meteoroid enters the Earth's atmosphere

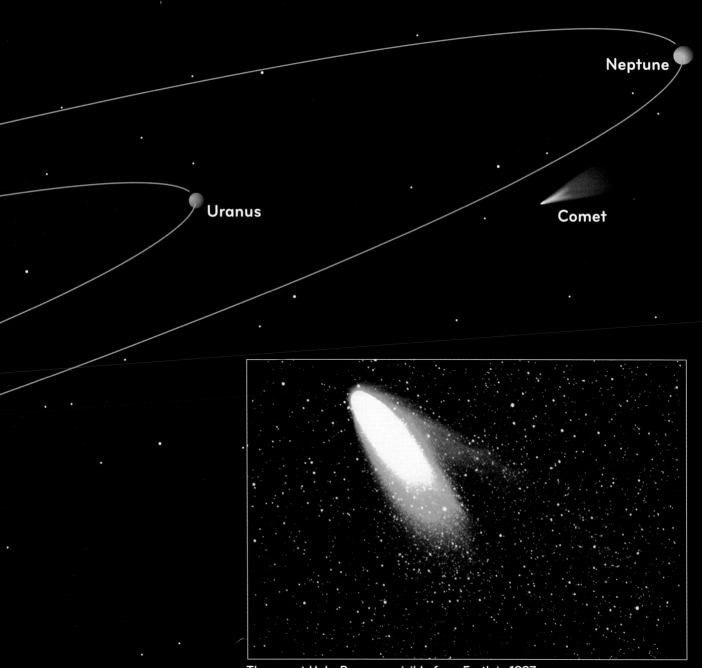

Neptune

Uranus

Comet

The comet Hale-Bopp was visible from Earth in 1997

The Sun
Our star

The Sun is the star of our Solar System.
It is a huge ball of scorching hot glowing
gases. Heat and light from this star
travel millions of kilometres to reach
Earth and support all life on our planet.
The Sun is large enough to contain
every single other object in the Solar
System. It is almost ten times wider
than the next largest object in the Solar
System, which is Jupiter.

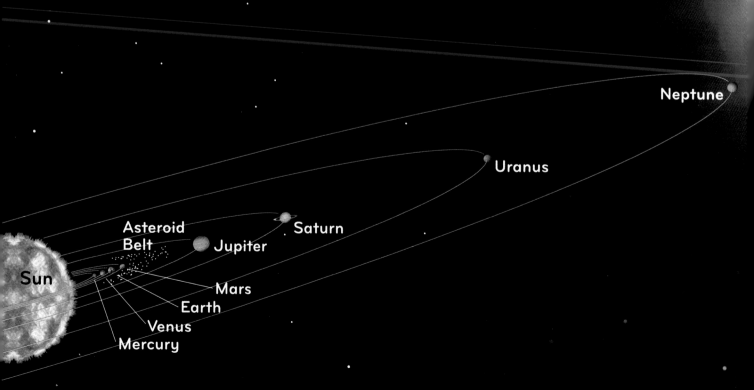

Neptune

Uranus

Asteroid
Belt

Saturn

Jupiter

Sun

Mars

Earth

Venus

Mercury

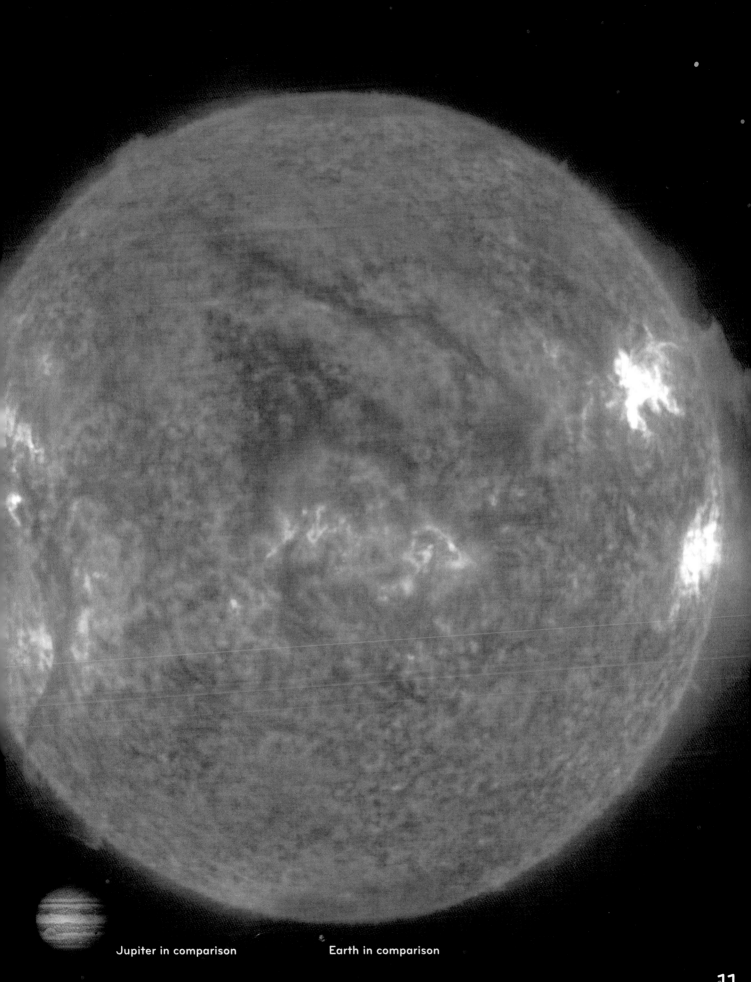

Jupiter in comparison   Earth in comparison

The Sun Facts

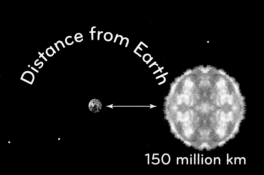

Distance from Earth

150 million km

Length of galactic year

230 million Earth years

Length of day

25 Earth days 9 hours

Diameter

1 391 016 km

Circumference

4 370 000 km

Average temperature

5504 °C

Age

4.6 billion years

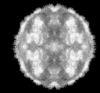

Sunspots are relatively cool, dark patches on the Sun's surface.
They come in many shapes and sizes and often appear in groups.
Sunspots can be over ten times the diameter of Earth.

Earth in comparison

A massive solar flare erupts from the Sun's surface

Inner Solar System

There are four inner planets: Mercury, Venus, Earth and Mars. They are closest to the Sun and are known as the terrestrial planets because their surfaces are solid and rocky. The four planets are very different from each other and their surfaces are dotted with impact craters, valleys and some volcanoes. The Asteroid Belt is a region beyond the orbit of Mars where thousands of asteroids are found orbiting the Sun.

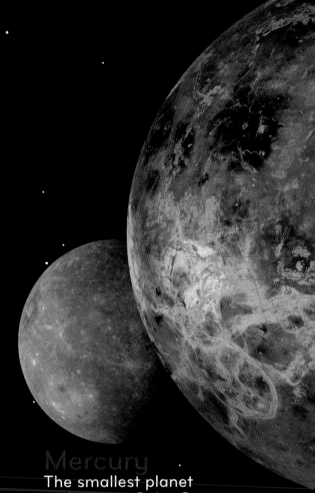

Mercury
The smallest planet in the Inner Solar System

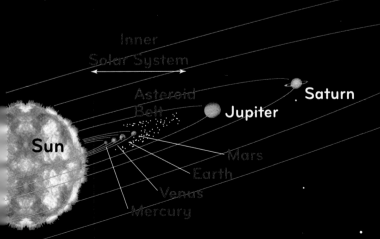

Neptune

Uranus

Saturn

Jupiter

Inner Solar System

Asteroid Belt

Mars

Earth

Venus

Mercury

Sun

Venus
Clouds of sulphuric acid prevent its surface being seen from Earth

Earth
The only planet in the Solar System known to have life

Ceres
The largest object in the Asteroid Belt

Mars
Named after the Roman god of war, it is often described as the "Red Planet"

Mercury

The closest planet to the Sun

Mercury is the smallest planet. It is closest to the Sun and takes only eighty-eight Earth days to complete an orbit of the Sun. Mercury is scorching hot on its sunlit side, however it has no atmosphere to retain this heat so temperatures on its unlit side are extremely cold.

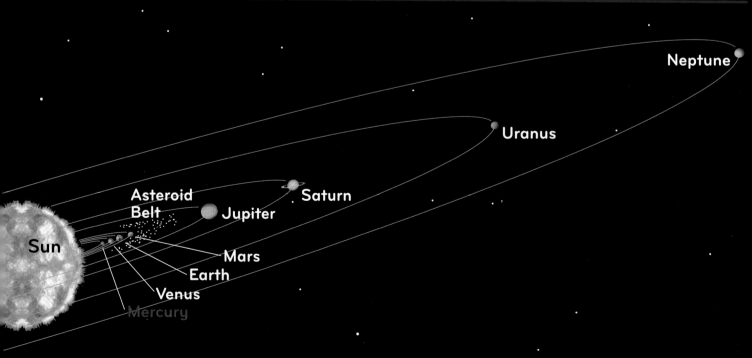

Neptune

Uranus

Saturn

Asteroid Belt

Jupiter

Sun

Mars

Earth

Venus

Mercury

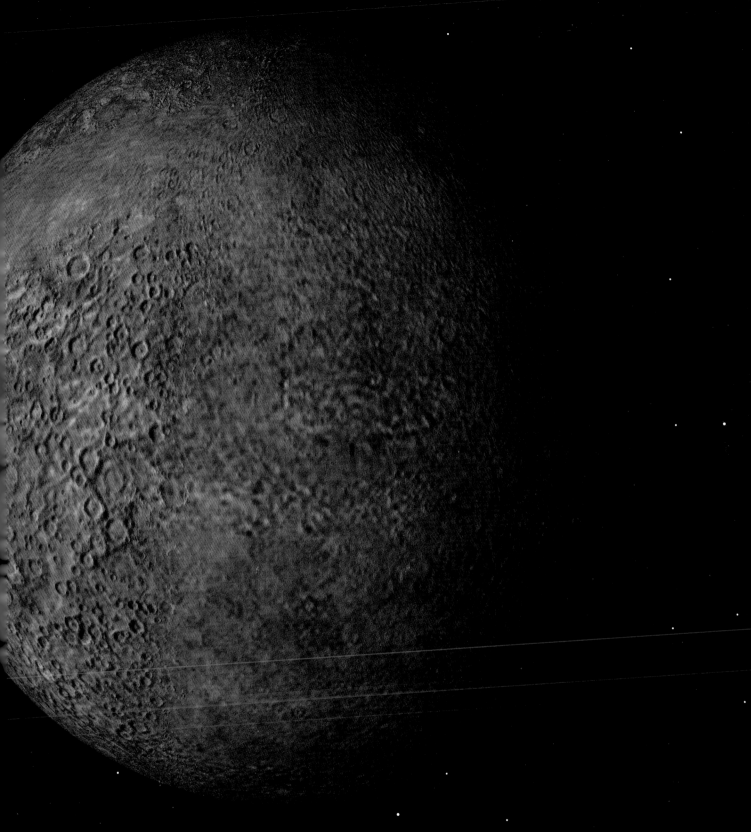

Cratered surface is evidence of
many asteroid and meteor impacts

Mercury and Earth compared

Mercury Facts

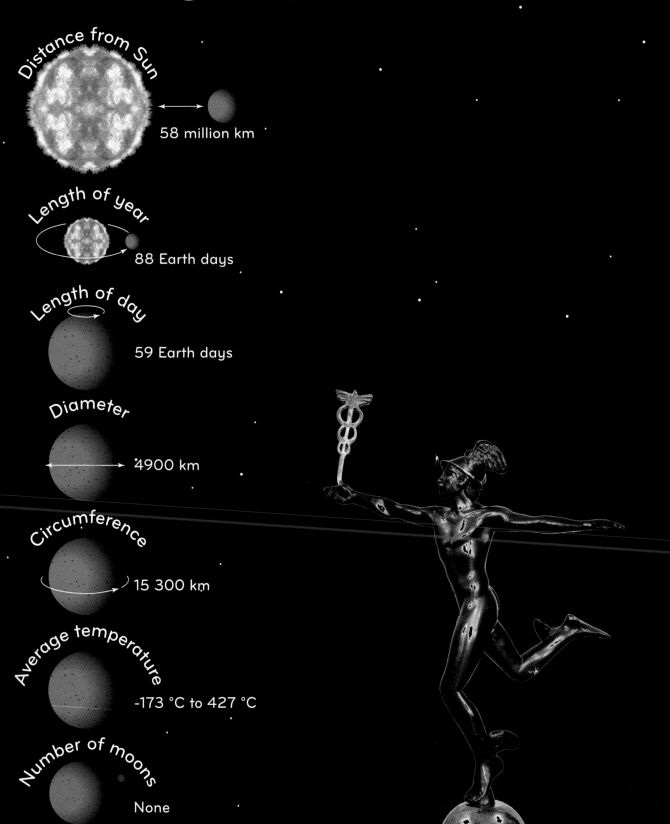

Distance from Sun
58 million km

Length of year
88 Earth days

Length of day
59 Earth days

Diameter
4900 km

Circumference
15 300 km

Average temperature
-173 °C to 427 °C

Number of moons
None

Mercury was named after the winged
messenger in Roman mythology

Van Eyck

Sophocles   •Vivaldi

Tolstoy

Michelangelo

Bach

Many of the craters on Mercury have been named after famous writers, musicians, painters and other artists

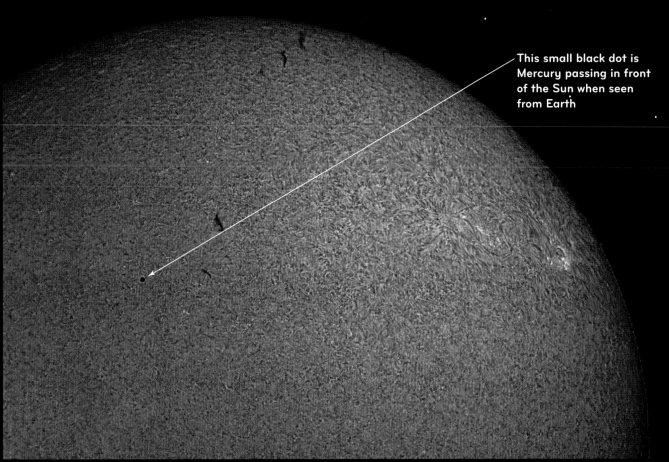

This small black dot is Mercury passing in front of the Sun when seen from Earth

Venus
Earth's neighbour

Venus is named after the Roman goddess of love and beauty because of its brightness and beauty in the night sky. It is the brightest object in the sky after the Sun and Earth's moon. It is the second planet from the Sun in the Solar System and the nearest planet to Earth. Venus is covered by a thick rapidly swirling atmosphere and temperatures are the hottest on any planet in the Solar System. The surface is covered by gently rolling hills and lava flows. There are not many mountains.

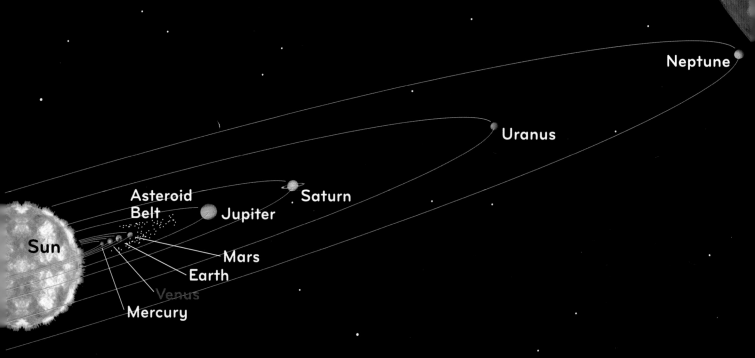

Neptune

Uranus

Saturn

Asteroid
Belt · Jupiter

Mars

Earth

Venus

Sun

Mercury

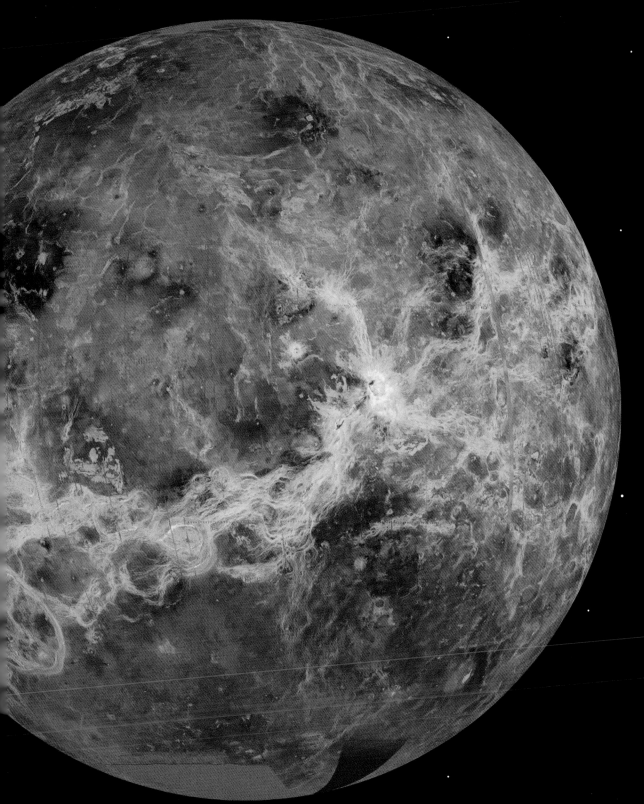

Venus's surface, shown in this image, is hidden
by dense clouds that contain sulphuric acid

Venus and Earth compared

Venus Facts

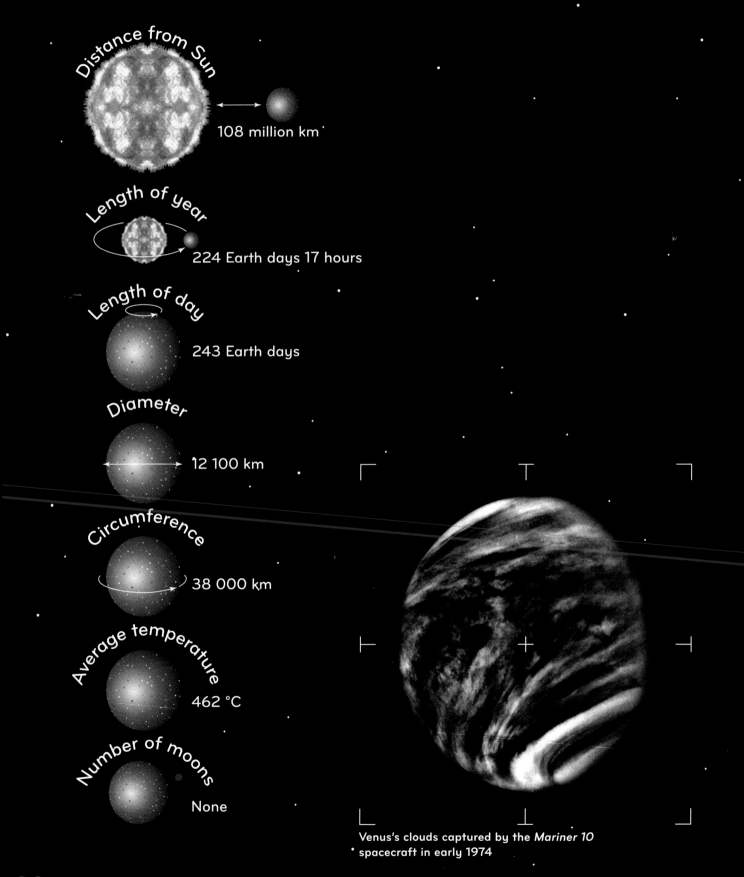

Distance from Sun

108 million km

Length of year

224 Earth days 17 hours

Length of day

243 Earth days

Diameter

12 100 km

Circumference

38 000 km

Average temperature

462 °C

Number of moons

None

Venus's clouds captured by the *Mariner 10* spacecraft in early 1974

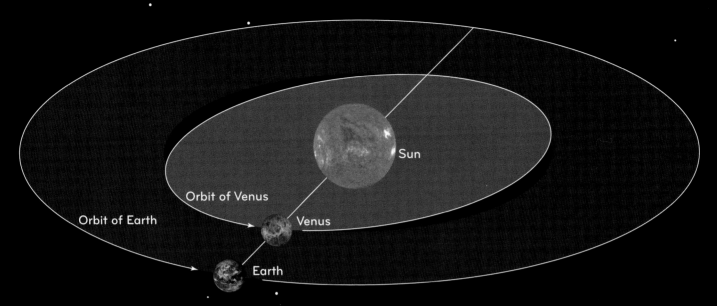

Venus's orbit is tilted in respect to the orbit of Earth

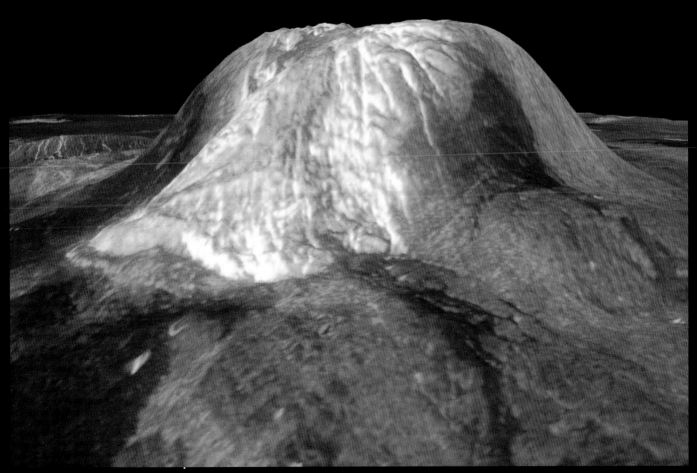

Gula Mons is a 3 km high volcano on the surface of Venus

Earth

Our home in space

Earth is the only planet in the Universe known to support life! It is a living planet, with plently of water, trees, plants and breathable air, protected by its atmosphere. It is the third planet from the Sun and is largest of the four rocky inner planets. Oceans, at least 4 kilometres deep, cover nearly 70 per cent of Earth's surface. It has one moon which is the only other place to be visited by people from Earth. It takes Earth 365 days and 6 hours (one year) to orbit the Sun.

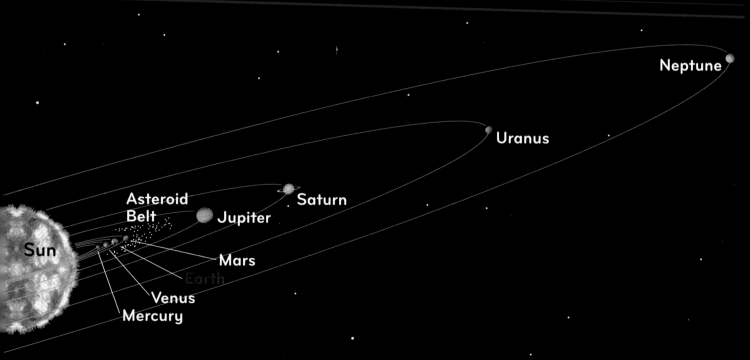

Neptune

Uranus

Saturn

Asteroid
Belt

Jupiter

Sun

Mars

Earth

Venus

Mercury

Earth is the third planet from the Sun and is home to millions of species, including humans

main layers called the crust, mantle, and core. The crust, the outermost layer, is rigid and very thin compared with the other two. Beneath the oceans, the crust varies little in thickness, generally extending only to about 5 kilometres. The thickness of the crust beneath continents is much more variable but averages at about 30 kilometres and under large mountain ranges, such as the Alps or the Sierra Nevada, the base of the crust can be as deep as 100 kilometres. The Earth's crust is brittle and can break. It is made up of separate pieces called plates. These are always moving and earthquakes often occur at the points where they meet.

hot layer of semi-solid rock approximately 2900 kilometres thick. At the centre of the Earth lies the core, the inner part of which is solid.

The structure of Earth

Crust
Mantle
Outer core
Inner core

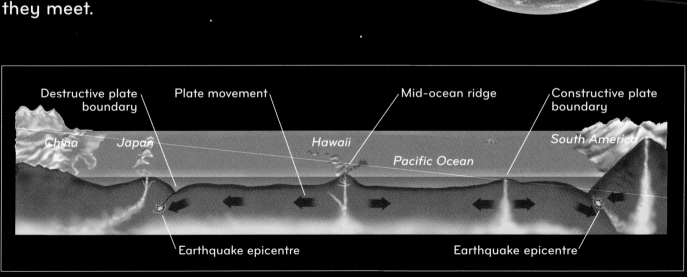

Destructive plate boundary
Plate movement
Mid-ocean ridge
Constructive plate boundary

China   Japan
Hawaii
South America

Pacific Ocean

Earthquake epicentre
Earthquake epicentre

A cross-section through the Pacific Ocean showing the plate structure

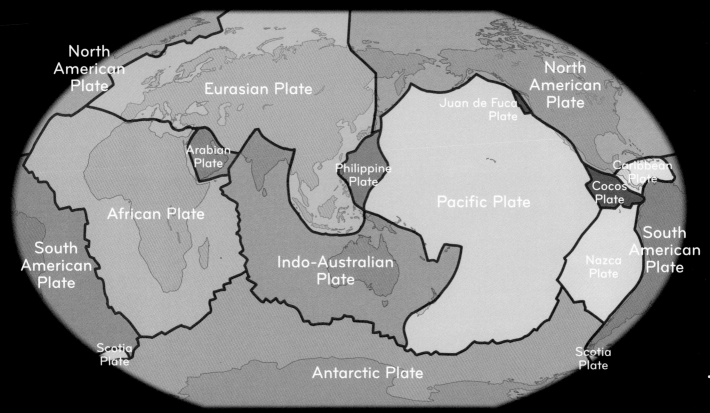

Earth's major plates

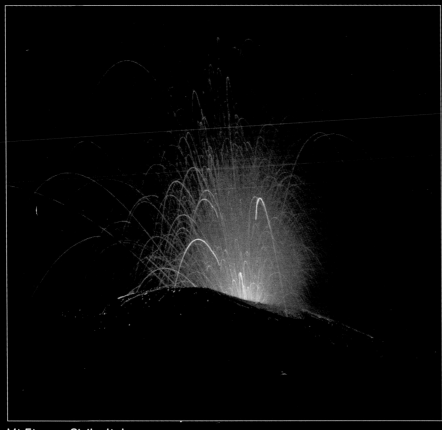

Mt Etna on Sicily, Italy

Loss of life in the ten most deadly earthquakes since 1900

Year	Location	Deaths
1976	China	255 000
2004	Indonesia/Indian Ocean	225 000
2010	Haiti	222 570
1920	China	200 000
1927	China	200 000
1923	Japan	142 807
1908	Italy	110 000
2005	Pakistan	74 648
1932	China	70 000
1970	Peru	66 794

Earth Facts

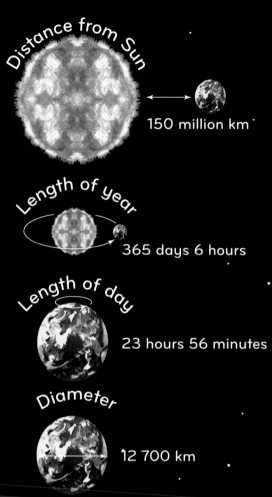

Distance from Sun

150 million km

Length of year

365 days 6 hours

Length of day

23 hours 56 minutes

Diameter

12 700 km

Circumference

40 000 km

Average temperature

15 °C

Number of moons

1

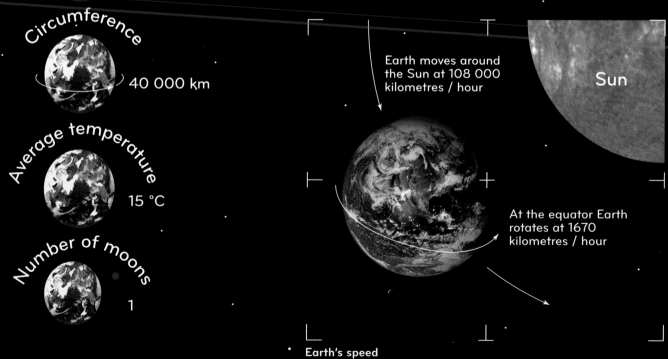

Earth moves around the Sun at 108 000 kilometres / hour

Sun

At the equator Earth rotates at 1670 kilometres / hour

Earth's speed

The effect of Earth's tilt

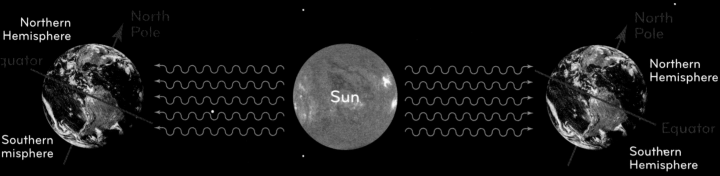

July
Summer in the
northern hemisphere

Northern
Hemisphere

North
Pole

Equator

Southern
Hemisphere

Sun

January
Summer in the
southern hemisphere

North
Pole

Northern
Hemisphere

Equator

Southern
Hemisphere

Summer is warmer than winter (in each hemisphere) because the Sun's rays hit the Earth at a more direct angle during summer than during winter and because the days are much longer than the nights during the summer. During the winter, the Sun's rays hit the Earth at an extreme angle, and the days are very short.

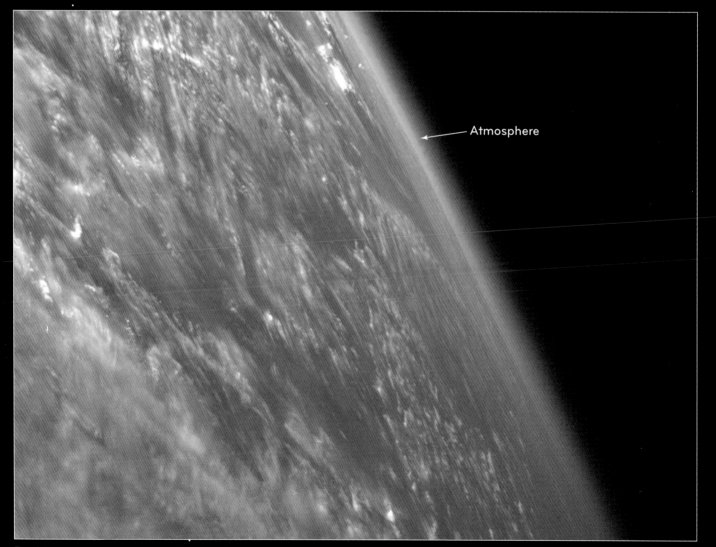

Atmosphere

Earth's atmosphere is about 450 km thick

Earth's companion
The Moon

The Moon is Earth's only natural satellite. It is the second brightest object in the sky after the Sun and is thought to have formed from the debris when a planet-sized object collided with Earth billions of years ago. It is the only object, other than Earth, to have been stepped on by human beings. Its Roman name is *Luna* and its Greek name is *Selene*. Although the Moon's appearance changes due to its phases, you are only ever able to see one side of it as it always faces Earth. There are a lot of dark patches on the moon which are flat areas of old lava flows which look like seas. The surface is very mountainous and there are peaks nearly as high as Mount Everest (the highest mountain on Earth).

The Moon's orbital plane is inclined in relation to the Earth's

Moon's orbit

Earth's orbit

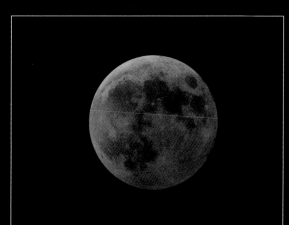

A lunar eclipse occurs when the Earth passes between the Sun and Moon

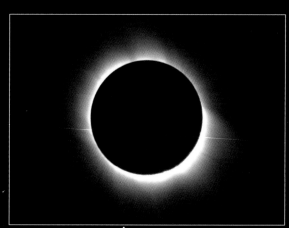

A solar eclipse occurs when the Moon passes between the Sun and Earth

The phases of the Moon

New moon	Waxing crescent	First quarter	Waxing gibbous	Full moon	Waning gibbous	Last quarter	Waning crescent	New moon

The new moon is not visible from Earth

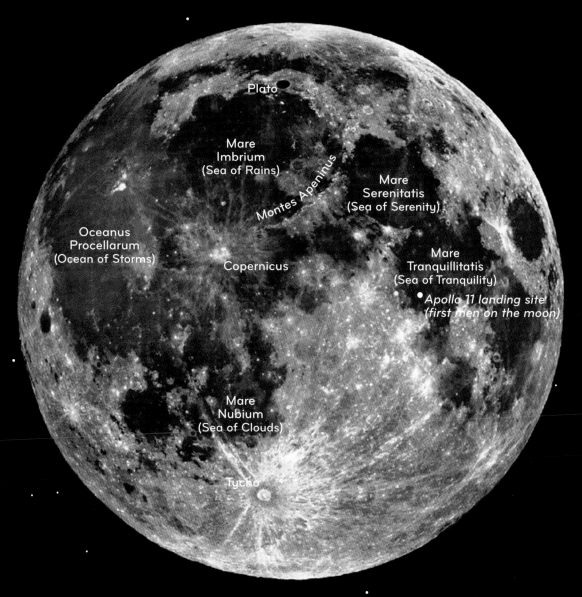

Plato

Mare Imbrium (Sea of Rains)

Montes Apeninus

Mare Serenitatis (Sea of Serenity)

Oceanus Procellarum (Ocean of Storms)

Copernicus

Mare Tranquillitatis (Sea of Tranquility)

●Apollo 11 landing site (first men on the moon)

Mare Nubium (Sea of Clouds)

Tycho

Only one side of the Moon is visible from Earth, the far side has only been seen by the few astronauts whose spaceships orbited it in the late 1960s and early 1970s.

The Moon and Earth compared

Mars
The red planet

Mars is the fourth planet from the Sun and because of its blood red colour has been named after the Roman god of war. Its surface has been affected by volcanoes, crustal movements and dust storms. Mars has the tallest mountain in the Solar System, Olympus Mons, which rises 24 kilometres above the surrounding land.

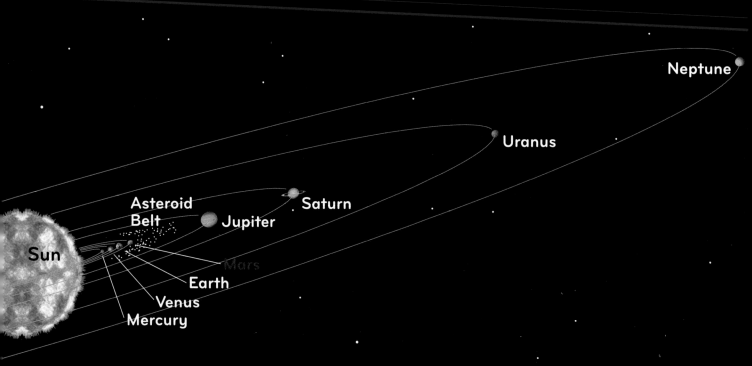

Neptune

Uranus

Saturn

Asteroid Belt

Jupiter

Sun

Mars

Earth

Venus

Mercury

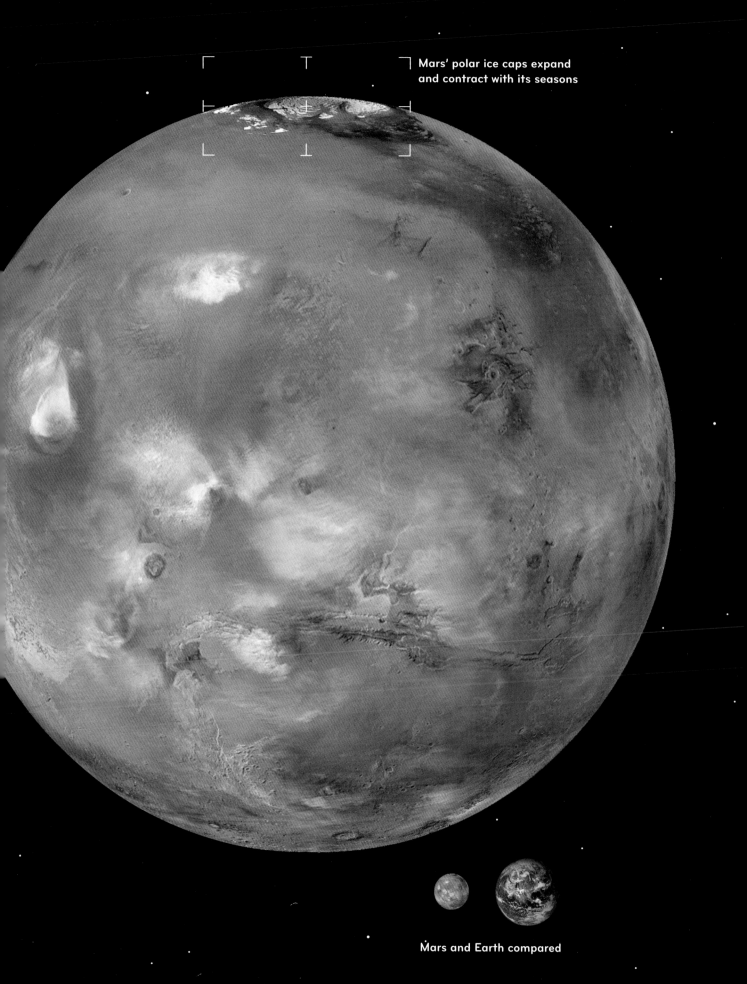

Mars' polar ice caps expand and contract with its seasons

Mars and Earth compared

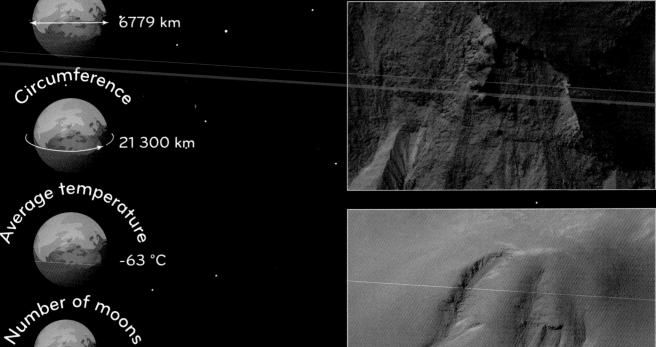

6779 km

Circumference 21 300 km

Average temperature -63 °C

Number of moons 2

Martian landscapes

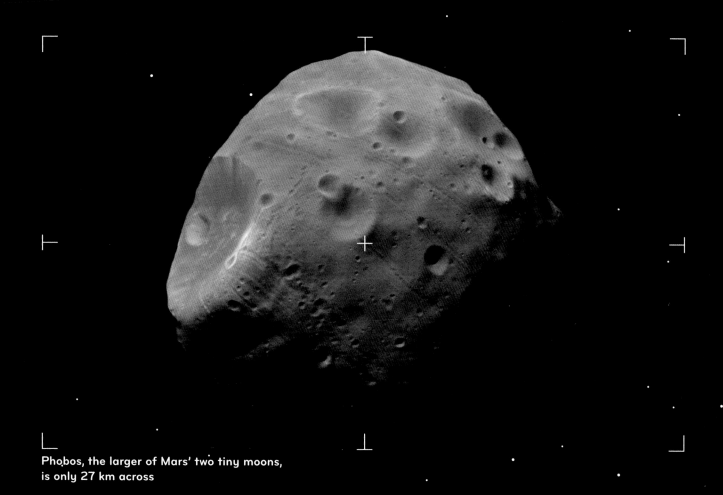

Phobos, the larger of Mars' two tiny moons, is only 27 km across

An image of Mars' surface taken by the *Mars Pathfinder Lander* in 1997

Asteroids

Asteroids are small lumps of rocks and ice which orbit the Sun like mini-planets. There are millions of asteroids, and like most other small bodies, asteroids are often thought to be the shattered remnants of objects within the young Solar System that never grew large enough to become planets.

Asteroids come in many shapes and sizes

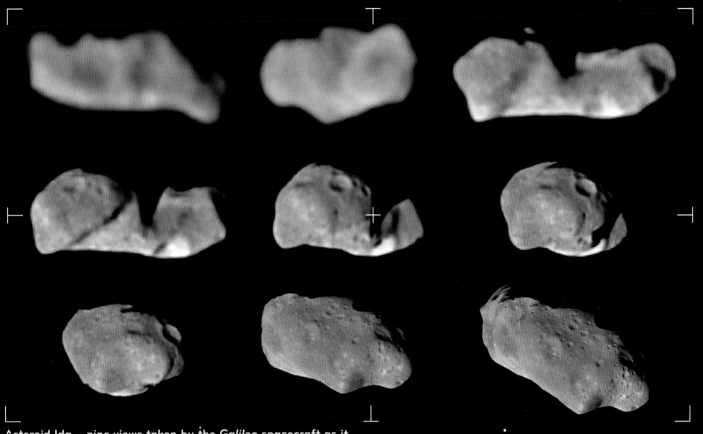

Asteroid Ida – nine views taken by the *Galileo* spacecraft as it
approached and passed the asteroid on 28 August, 1993

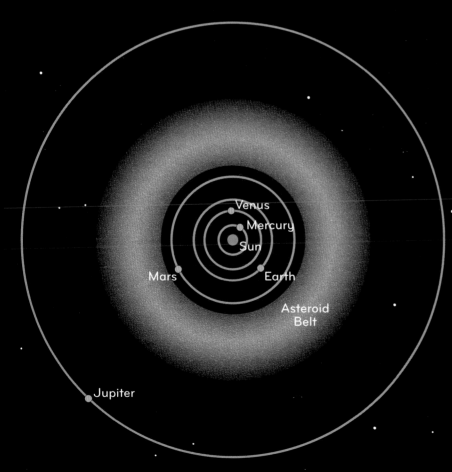

The Asteroid Belt is a concentration
of asteroids orbiting the Sun
between the orbits of Mars and
Jupiter, closer to the orbit of Mars.
Most asteroids orbit from between
300 million to 600 million
kilometres from the Sun. The
asteroids in the Asteroid Belt have
slightly elliptical orbits. The time for
one revolution around the Sun
varies from about three to six
Earth years.

Outer Solar System

The outer planets are: Jupiter, Saturn, Uranus and Neptune. They are sometimes known as the Gas Giants as they are huge in comparison to the inner planets and, made up mostly of gas, do not have solid surfaces. All four have rings around them, with Saturn's being the most famous. The four planets also have large numbers of moons orbiting them.

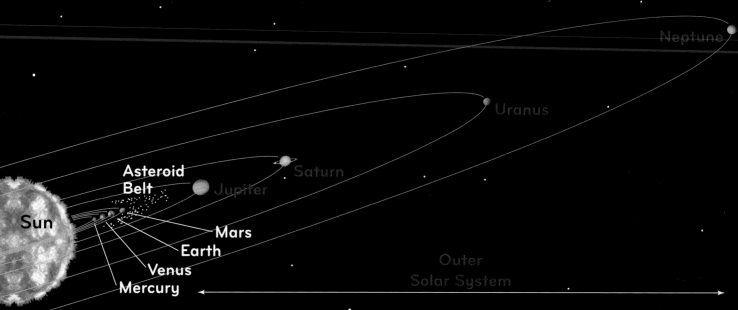

Neptune

Uranus

Saturn

Jupiter

Asteroid
Belt

Sun

Mars
Earth
Venus
Mercury

Outer
Solar System

Jupiter
The fifth planet from the Sun
and the largest planet

Saturn
The rings of Saturn may be less
than 10 metres thick in places

Uranus
Uranus was the
first planet discovered
with a telescope

Neptune
Named for the Roman
god of the sea, it is the
fourth-largest planet

39

Jupiter
The giant planet

Jupiter is the largest planet in the
Solar System. It is more than 300
times bigger than Earth. The planet is
the fourth brightest object visible from
Earth after the Sun, the Earth's moon
and Venus. Its main feature is a Great
Red Spot, which is a storm that has
been going on for years. Jupiter has
a ring system like all of the large gas
planets, although these rings are not
as famous or as visible as Saturn's.
Orbiting Jupiter are at least
sixty-three moons.

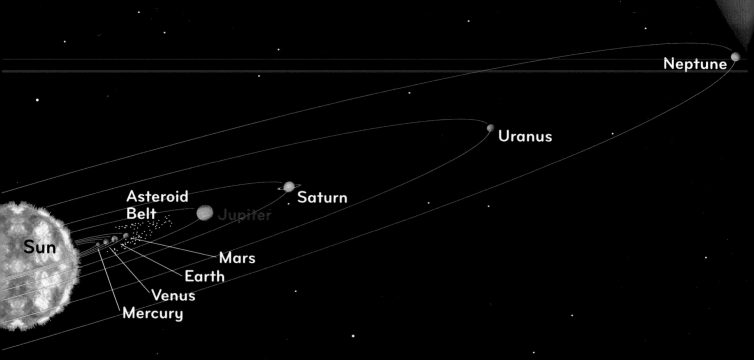

Neptune

Uranus

Asteroid
Belt
Saturn
Jupiter
Sun
Mars
Earth
Venus
Mercury

Great Red Spot

Shadow of one
of Jupiter's moons

Earth in comparison

Jupiter's moons

The Sun is a star with eight planets orbiting it. Jupiter also seems to have its very own solar system with at least sixty-three very different moons orbiting it. Most of these moons are very small and are probably asteroids caught by Jupiter's strong gravitational pull to remain in orbit around the planet. The four largest moons, Io, Europa, Ganymede and Callisto are like little worlds, each different from each other. They are known as the Galilean satellites and can be seen with the aid of binoculars.

An image of the mountains and volcanoes on Io taken by the *Galileo* spacecraft in 1999

Jupiter and the four moons discovered in 1610 by Galileo Galilei

Io, with over 400 active volcanoes, is the most geologically active object in the Solar System

Ganymede is the largest moon in the Solar System and is larger than the planet Mercury.

Europa is the smallest of the Galilean moons and orbits Jupiter in just over three and a half days

Thebe, one of Jupiter's smallest moons, is about 100 km across and takes just over 16 hours to orbit Jupiter

Callisto has one of the most heavily cratered surfaces in the Solar System

Jupiter Facts

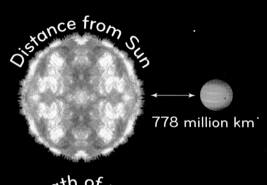

Distance from Sun

778 million km

Length of year

11 Earth years 314 days

Length of day

9 hours 56 minutes

Diameter

143 000 km

Circumference

450 000 km

Average temperature

-148 °C

Number of moons

63

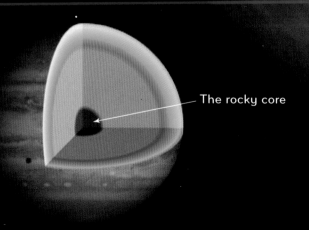

The rocky core

Interior of Jupiter

Jupiter's Great Red Spot with Earth in comparison

Saturn
The ringed planet

Saturn is the second largest planet in the Solar System. It is often called the ringed planet because it is surrounded by rings of dust and rocks. Like Jupiter Saturn is a gas giant and is made up mainly of hydrogen. It is very light and if placed in a big pond of water it would float. Saturn spins very quickly. It takes only ten hours to rotate fully. A year on Saturn would take almost thirty Earth years. However, a day on Saturn is about ten and a half hours.

Neptune

Uranus

Asteroid
Belt

Saturn

Jupiter

Sun

Mars

Earth

Venus

Mercury

Saturn's rings are one of the most spectacular
and beautiful sights in the Solar System

Earth in comparison

Saturn's rings

Saturn's rings are probably the most distinguishing feature of any planet in the Solar System. The width of the planet is 116 500 kilometres, but the rings surrounding it increase this width to around 270 000 kilometres. The rings are about one kilometre thick and are made up of particles ranging in size from specks of dust to massive icy boulders.

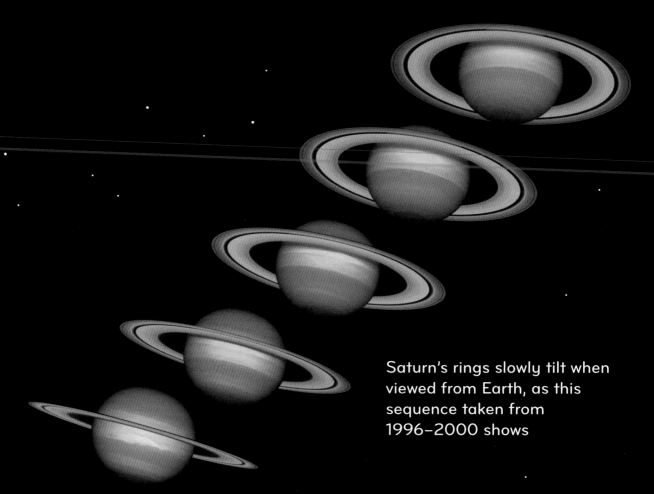

Saturn's rings slowly tilt when viewed from Earth, as this sequence taken from 1996–2000 shows

Saturn's rings are so narrow they practically disappear when 'edge' on

Saturn's rings are divided into eight major ring divisions.
Each ring orbits at a different speed around the planet

Saturn's moons

Orbiting Saturn are at least sixty-two moons. Most of these moons are quite small. However, 1 221 860 kilometres away from Saturn is the second biggest moon in the Solar System: Titan. Titan is an extremely interesting moon. It is the only moon in the Solar System to have an atmosphere which is made up mainly of nitrogen. Some hydrocarbons present in Titan's atmosphere make it appear an orange colour.

This image shows the giant moon Titan behind
Saturn's rings and the tiny moon Epimetheus

Hyperion is the largest
irregularly shaped
moon ever observed

Mimas has a large
crater almost one-third
of its diameter ·

Pheobe orbits Saturn in
the opposite direction to
· most other moons

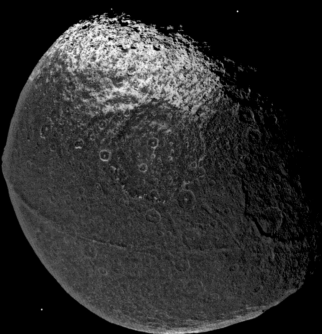

Iapetus has a
mountain ridge
over 20 km high

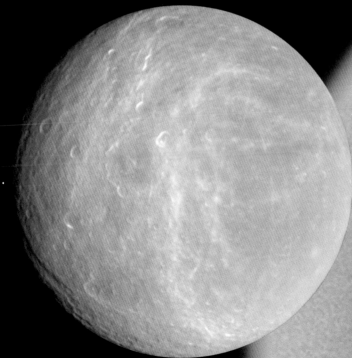

Rhea is Saturn's
second-largest moon

Titan is Saturn's largest moon
and the second-largest in the
Solar System

Saturn Facts

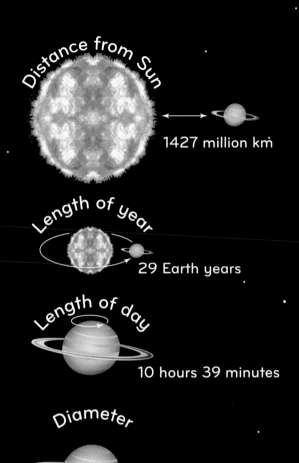

Distance from Sun

1427 million km

Length of year

29 Earth years

Length of day

10 hours 39 minutes

Diameter

116 500 km

Circumference

366 000 km

Average temperature

-178 °C

Number of moons

62

The bright feature on this image is a storm on Saturn's surface with an estimated speed of over 1500 km per hour

Saturn is more than twice the distance away from Earth as Jupiter

Earth

Jupiter

Saturn

629 million km

1277 million km

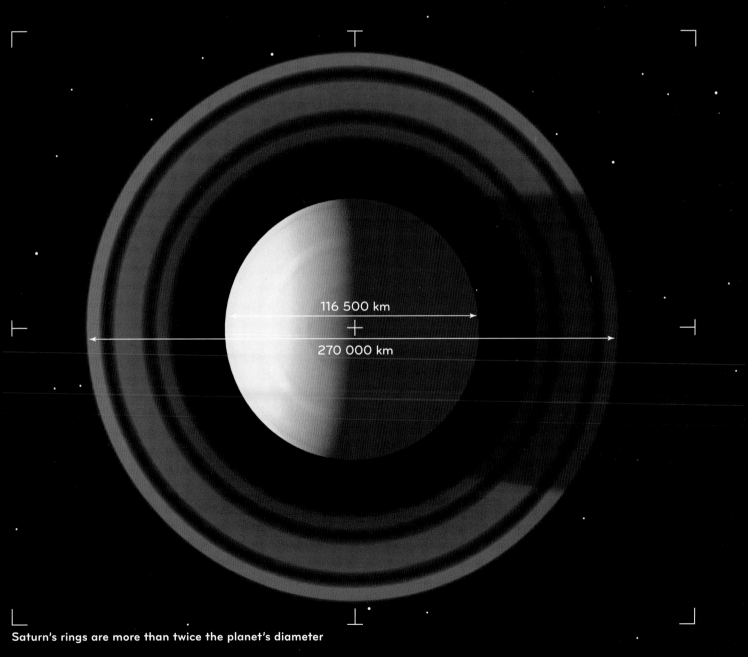

116 500 km

270 000 km

Saturn's rings are more than twice the planet's diameter

Uranus
The blue planet

Uranus was first identified as a planet in 1781 by the British astronomer William Herschel. Uranus orbits the Sun on its side. This tipped rotational axis gives rise to extreme seasons on Uranus. It is thought that its unusual spin is due to a collision with another planet-sized object millions of years ago.

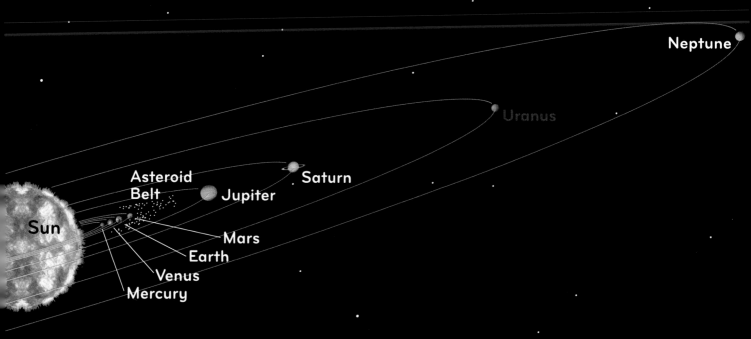

Neptune

Uranus

Asteroid
Belt

Saturn

Jupiter

Sun

Mars

Earth

Venus

Mercury

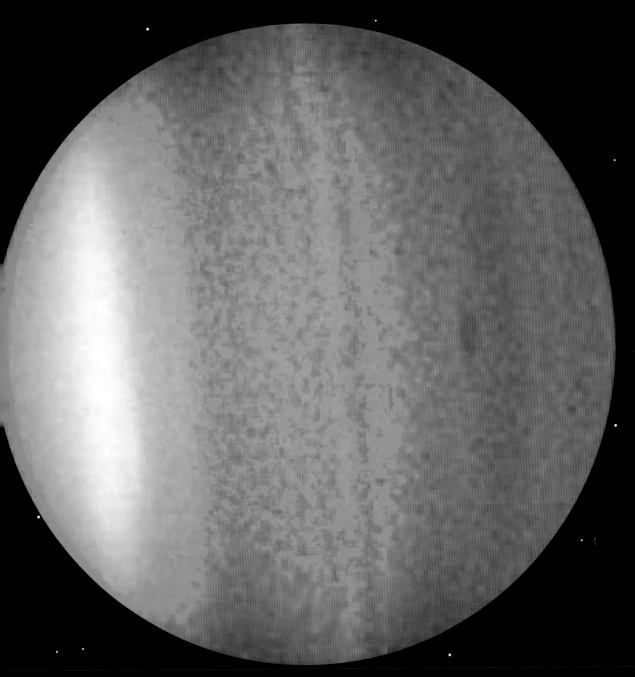

This 2006 image taken by the *Hubble Space Telescope* shows bands and a dark spot in Uranus's atmosphere

Earth in comparison

Uranus Facts

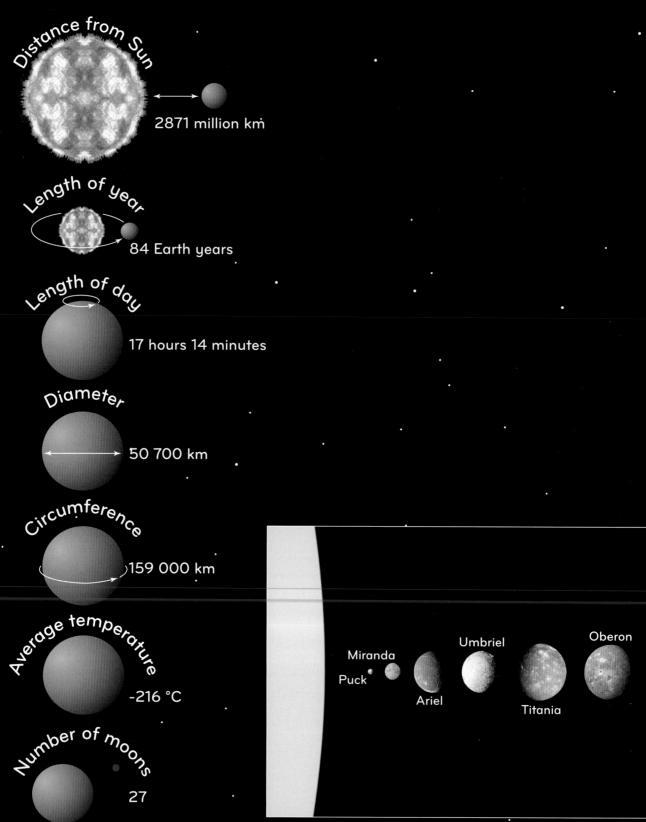

Distance from Sun
2871 million km

Length of year
84 Earth years

Length of day
17 hours 14 minutes

Diameter
50 700 km

Circumference
159 000 km

Average temperature
-216 °C

Number of moons
27

Miranda
Puck
Ariel
Umbriel
Titania
Oberon

The six largest moons of Uranus are named after characters
from the works of William Shakespeare and Alexander Pope

The extreme seasons on Uranus

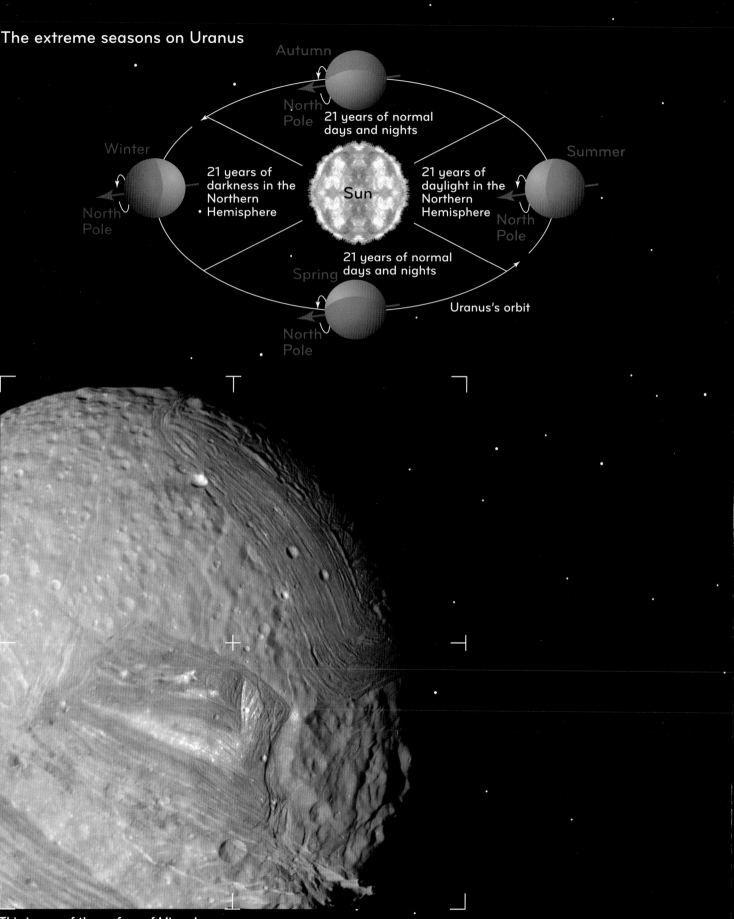

Autumn

North Pole

21 years of normal days and nights

Winter

Summer

21 years of darkness in the Northern Hemisphere

North Pole

Sun

21 years of daylight in the Northern Hemisphere

North Pole

North Pole

21 years of normal days and nights

Spring

Uranus's orbit

North Pole

This image of the surface of Miranda displays many different geological features

Neptune
The furthest planet

Named after the Roman god of the sea, probably because of its deep blue colour, Neptune is also the windiest planet in the Solar System. It spins once every sixteen hours. Orbiting Neptune are at least thirteen moons and a ring system. Several dark spots have been seen on Neptune. The largest is about the size of Earth and is known as the Great Dark Spot. It may be a huge storm like the Great Red Spot on Jupiter. In the 1990s the spot vanished and another appeared in a new location.

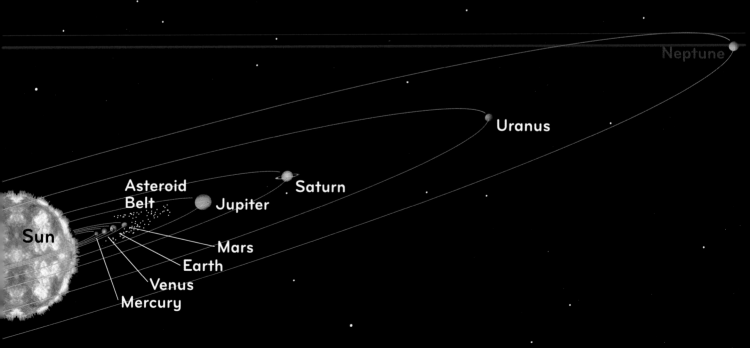

Neptune

Uranus

Saturn

Asteroid
Belt

Jupiter

Mars

Earth

Venus

Mercury

Sun

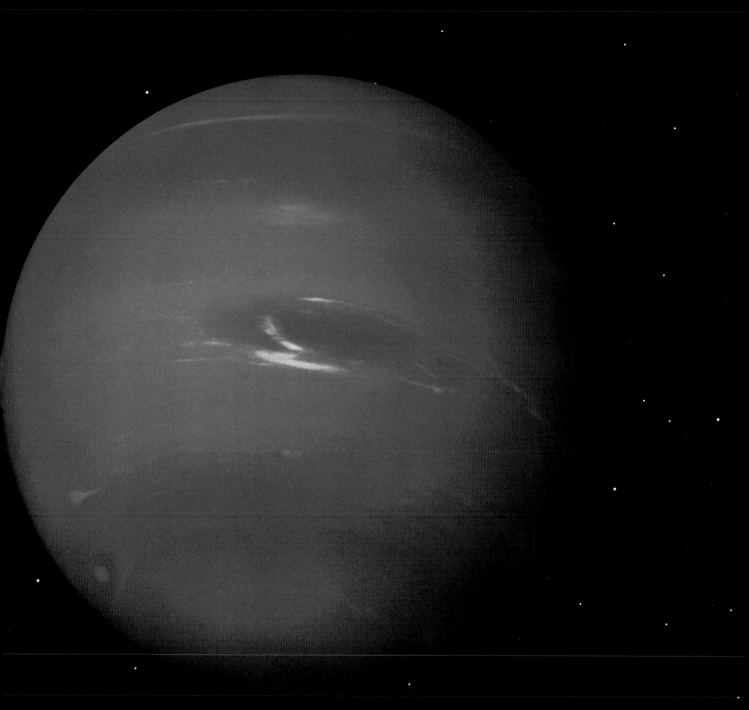

Neptune is the last of the Gas Giants in the
Solar System and is more than thirty times
as far from the Sun as Earth

Earth in comparison

Neptune Facts

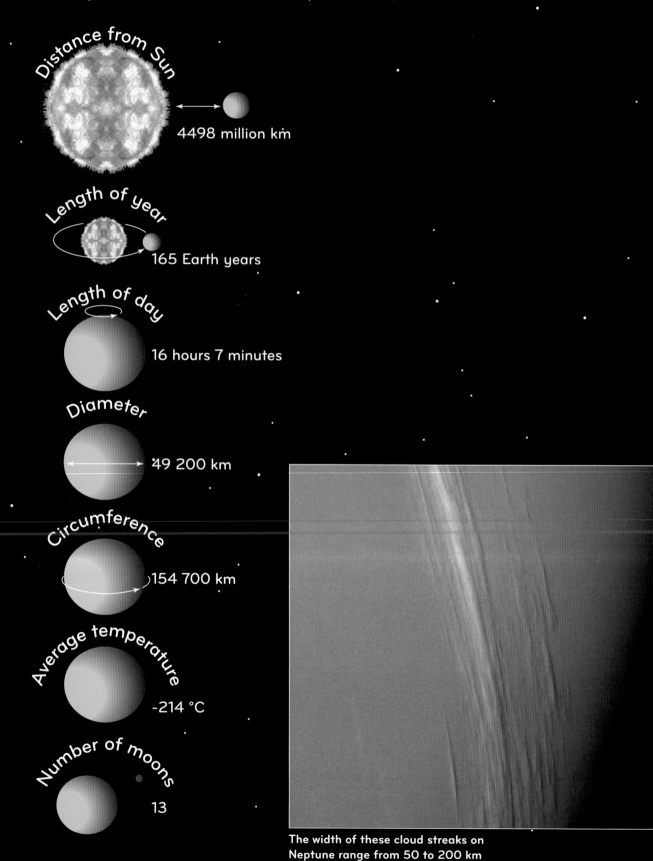

Distance from Sun

4498 million km

Length of year

165 Earth years

Length of day

16 hours 7 minutes

Diameter

49 200 km

Circumference

154 700 km

Average temperature

-214 °C

Number of moons

13

The width of these cloud streaks on
Neptune range from 50 to 200 km

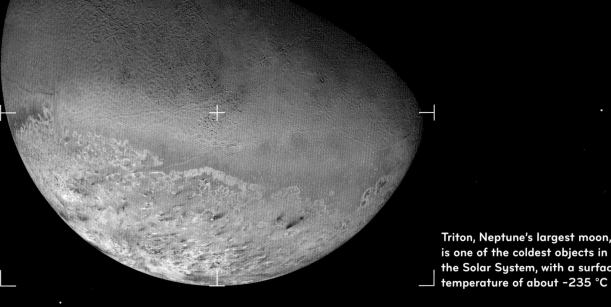

Triton, Neptune's largest moon, is one of the coldest objects in the Solar System, with a surface temperature of about −235 °C

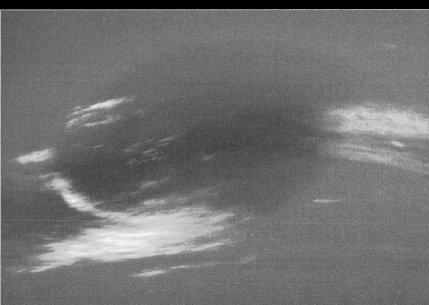

The winds near the Great Dark Spot on Neptune have been measured to be about 2400 km per hour

Neptune is thirty times the distance away from the Sun than Earth

Sun

Earth

Neptu

150 million km

4498 million km

Pluto
The dwarf planet

Pluto was discovered in 1930. For a
long time it was thought to be the ninth
and furthest planet from the Sun. In
2006 it was reclassified as a dwarf
planet. Pluto has four moons orbiting
it. Charon, the largest, was discovered
in 1978 and is almost as large as Pluto.
The two objects appear to spin around
each other, taking six days to complete
a full orbit. Photographs of Pluto
suggest that it has a surface of frozen
gas and may have a thin atmosphere.

Pluto

Neptune

Uranus

Saturn

Asteroid
Belt

Jupiter

Sun

Mars

Earth

Venus

Mercury

Pluto is so small and distant that the task
of seeing the surface is as challenging as trying
to see the markings on a football 40 miles away.

Pluto and Earth compared

Pluto Facts

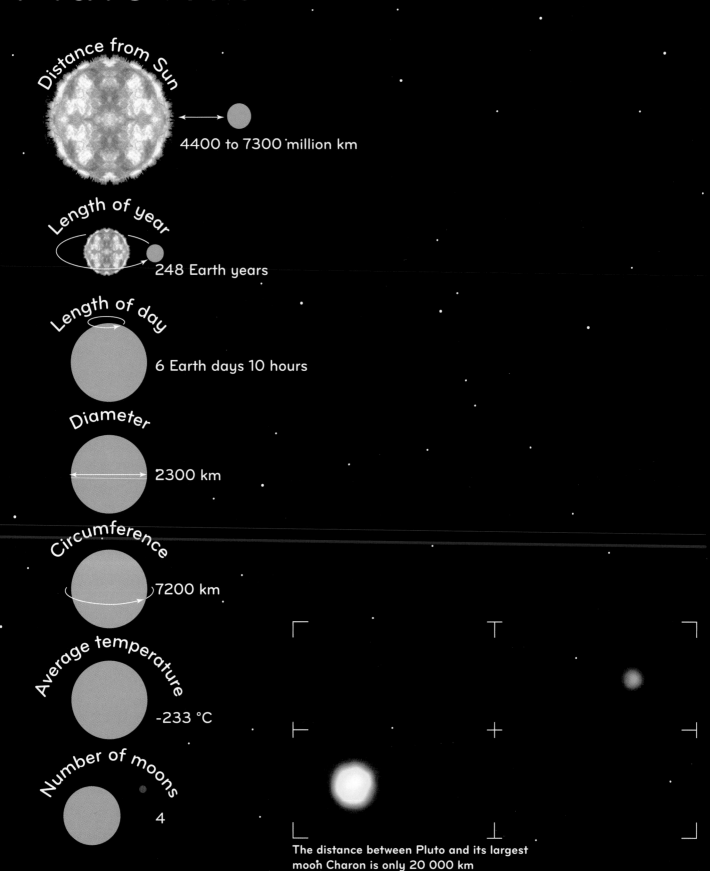

Distance from Sun
4400 to 7300 million km

Length of year
248 Earth years

Length of day
6 Earth days 10 hours

Diameter
2300 km

Circumference
7200 km

Average temperature
-233 °C

Number of moons
4

The distance between Pluto and its largest moon Charon is only 20 000 km

Pluto superimposed on a map of the United States of America

Pluto's orbit is so eccentric there are times
when it is closer to the Sun than Neptune

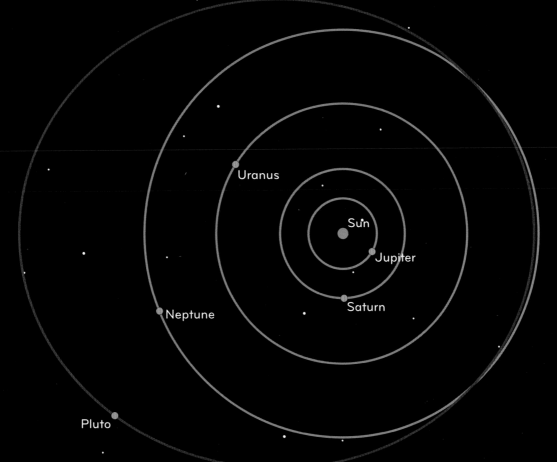

Comets

Comets are balls of rock and dirty ice
that grow tails as they approach the
Sun. They have oval shaped orbits and
only come near to the Sun for a very
short time. The solid part, the nucleus,
of a comet is surrounded by glowing
gases, the coma, which stretches out
into a tail. Some comets have more
than one tail, a bluish one which trails
behind the comet and a yellowish one
which follows the path of the comets
orbit. Bright comets can only be seen
from Earth once every ten years and
those with long orbits may only be
seen every few thousand years.

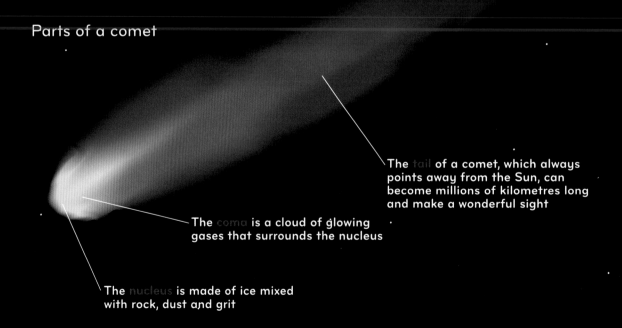

Parts of a comet

The tail of a comet, which always
points away from the Sun, can
become millions of kilometres long
and make a wonderful sight

The coma is a cloud of glowing
gases that surrounds the nucleus

The nucleus is made of ice mixed
with rock, dust and grit

Comet McNaught and the setting sun over the Pacific Ocean on 1 January, 2007

Man and space

Sputnik 1

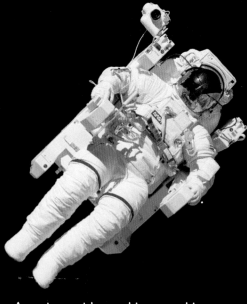

An astronaut leaves his spaceship

1957	The first artificial satellite, *Sputnik 1*, launched
1959	First photograph of Earth from orbit
1961	First man in space
1963	First woman in space
1965	First space walk
1966	First spacecraft to land on the Moon
1969	Man lands on the Moon

1980	*Voyager 1* passes Saturn
1981	First Space Shuttle launch
1986	Space Shuttle *Challenger* disaster
1986	*Voyager 2* passes Uranus
1989	*Voyager 2* passes Neptune

| **1957 – 1969** | **1970 – 1979** | **1980 – 1989** |

1970	First lunar rover
1971	First space station
1972	Last man on the moon
1975	First images of Venus
1976	First images of Mars
1977	Voyager spacecrafts launched
1979	First images of Jupiter and Saturn

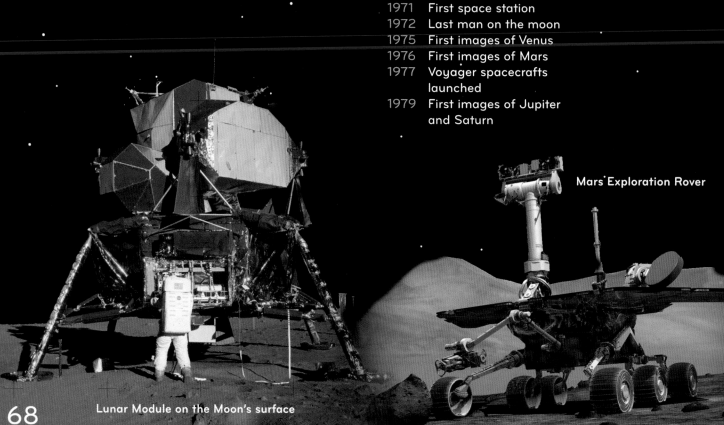

Mars Exploration Rover

Lunar Module on the Moon's surface

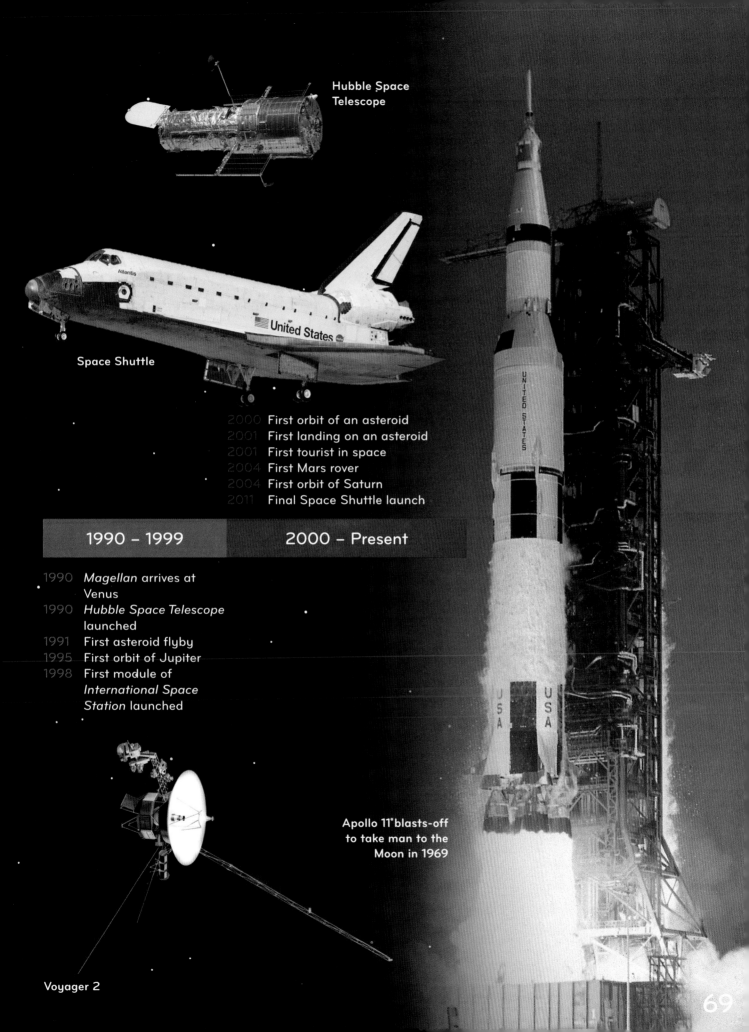

Hubble Space
Telescope

Space Shuttle

Atlantis

United States

2000 First orbit of an asteroid
2001 First landing on an asteroid
2001 First tourist in space
2004 First Mars rover
2004 First orbit of Saturn
2011 Final Space Shuttle launch

1990 – 1999

2000 – Present

1990 *Magellan* arrives at
      Venus
1990 *Hubble Space Telescope*
      launched
1991 First asteroid flyby
1995 First orbit of Jupiter
1998 First module of
      *International Space
      Station* launched

Apollo 11 blasts-off
to take man to the
Moon in 1969

Voyager 2

Solar System at a glance

Name	Diameter	Circumference	Distance from Sun	Average temperature
Sun	1 391 016 km	4 370 000 km	...	5504 °C
Mercury	4900 km	15 300 km	58 million km	-173 °C to 427 °C
Venus	12 100 km	38 000 km	108 million km	462 °C
Earth	12 700 km	40 000 km	150 million km	15 °C
Mars	6779 km	21 300 km	228 million km	-63 °C
Jupiter	143 000 km	450 000 km	778 million km	-148 °C
Saturn	116 500 km	366 000 km	1427 million km	-178 °C
Uranus	50 700 km	159 000 km	2871 million km	-216 °C
Neptune	49 200 km	154 700 km	4498 million km	-214 °C
Pluto	2300 km	7 200 km	4400 to 7300 million km	-233 °C

Length of year	Length of day	Number of moons	Symbol
...	25 Earth days 9 hours		☉
88 Earth days	59 Earth days	none	☿
224 Earth days 17 hours	243 Earth days	none	♀
365 days 6 hours	23 hours 56 mins	1	⊕
687 Earth days	24 hours 37 mins	2	♂
11 Earth years 314 days	9 hours 55 mins	63	♃
29 Earth years	10 hours 39 mins	62	♄
84 Earth years	17 hours 14 mins	27	♅
165 Earth years	16 hours 7 mins	13	♆
248 Earth years	6 Earth days 10 hours	4	♇

Quiz 1

1 The Solar System includes

- 5 planets
- 10 planets
- 8 planets
- 12 planets

2 Which planet has the shortest orbit?

- Earth
- Mercury
- Venus
- Neptune

3 Which planet in the Solar System has rings?

- Saturn
- Uranus
- Neptune
- All of the above

Answers at the back of the book

4 Which planet is furthest from the Sun?

- Earth
- Neptune
- Saturn
- Mars

5 How many moons does Mars have?

- 3
- 2
- 63
- 27

6 How long does it take for Earth to orbit the Sun?

- 365 days 6 hours
- 165 years
- 88 days
- 84 years

1 Which planet can
support life?

● Neptune
● Venus
● Earth
● All of the above

2 Which planet is nearest
the Sun?

● Neptune
● Mars
● Earth
● Mercury

3 Which planet is made up
mostly of gases?

● Mercury
● Earth
● Jupiter
● Venus

4 Which planet is referred to as the Red Planet?

- Venus
- Mars
- Earth
- Uranus

5 Which is the largest planet in the Solar System?

- Earth
- Mercury
- Venus
- Jupiter

6 Which planet is named after the Roman goddess of love?

- Venus
- Saturn
- Earth
- Jupiter

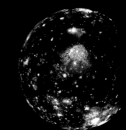

Answers at the back of the book

Glossary

anti-clockwise	The direction that the majority of the objects move in our Solar System.
asteroid	An object made up of rocks and metal, that orbits a star and is found in space.
astronomer	Someone who studies space, including the planets, stars, galaxies, comets and astronomy.
atmosphere	The layer of gases surrounding the surface of a planet, moon or star.
circumference	A measurement taken around the fattest, middle part of a planet.
comet	Small ball of dirty ice, dust and gas which orbits the Sun (often in oval orbits). Comets are only visible from Earth when they are close enough to the Sun to start burning off their dust/gas. Some comets take a few decades to complete an orbit, others take thousands of years. Some comets are also known to orbit Jupiter.
core	The centre of a space object, such as a planet, moon, or star.
crater	A bowl-shaped depression on the surface of a planet, moon or asteroid formed when a meteorite or another asteroid hits the surface.
crust	The thin rocky outer surface of a planet or moon.
day	Length of time it takes for a planet to completely rotate on its axis.
dwarf planet	A rounded body orbiting the Sun. Pluto, Ceres and Eris are examples of dwarf planets.
equator	An imaginery line running around the middle of a planet.
galaxy	A large group of stars, bound together by gravity.
Gas Giant	A type of planet with small, dense cores that do not have a solid surface, rather they are made of of gas and liquids. Examples include Jupiter, Saturn, Uranus and Neptune.
gravity	The force that pulls our Universe together.
inner planets	Those planets closest to the Sun, known as Mercury, Venus, Earth and Mars.
lava flow	Refers to moving molten rock expelled from a volcano. Only Earth and Io (a moon of Jupiter) currently have active volcanoes in our Solar System.
mantle	The area surrounding the core of a rocky planet.
Milky Way	The spiral galaxy, containing over 100 billion stars creating a broad band of light in the night sky, in which our Solar System is located.

moon	Any mini-planet which orbits another planet.
orbit	The path of one object as it revolves around another object. For example, the planets orbit, or travel around the Sun.
outer planets	Those planets in our Solar System, furthest from the Sun, beyond the asteroid belt, which includes Jupiter, Saturn, Uranus and Neptune.
planet	A large object or ball made up of rock or gas, which orbits a star and has a solid core. There are eight planets in our Solar System.
planetoid	Another term for asteroids, which are also called mini-planets.
plates	The Earth's solid surface is broken up into moving pieces or plates. It is the only planet in the Solar System to have active plates.
pole	Planets have two poles, which are the furthest points away from its equator.
rotate	Planets spin around their central axis. Earth rotates about its axis every 24 hours.
satellite	Any object in outer space that goes around another object. For example, the Moon is a satellite of Earth or man-made satellites orbit the Earth.
solar	The latin term 'Sol' translates to Sun, so solar refers to anything related to the Sun.
Solar System	The group of eight planets, and other objects, such as moons, ice and rocks, that all orbit around the Sun.
spiral galaxy	A galaxy often forms a circular shape, whereby the stars, gas and dust are gathered in long spiral arms winding outward from the galaxy's centre.
star	A ball of exploding gas held together by its own gravity.
Sun	A medium-sized yellow star at the centre of our Solar System, with a diameter 100 times that of Earth.
tail	A tail or a coma is the visible dust and gas that melts off a comet as it passes by the Sun. It is blown away from the Sun by the solar winds.
terrestrial planet	Planets mostly made up of rock, such as the four planets of the inner Solar System (Mercury, Venus, Earth, and Mars).
year	The length of time it takes a planet to go around the Sun. Earth's year lasts 365 days 6 hours.

Index

Quiz answers

Quiz 1 (page 72)

1	8 planets	4	Neptune
2	Mercury	5	2
3	All of the above	6	365 days 6 hours

Quiz 2 (page 74)

1	Earth	4	Mars
2	Mercury	5	Jupiter
3	Jupiter	6	Venus